# Brooke & Ki

Brooke Gantt

## BROOKE & KI

© 2017 Brooke Gantt

All rights reserved.

No part of this book may be reproduced or stored in a retrieval system, or transmitted in any form or by any means, electronic, mechanical, photocopying, recording, or otherwise, without written permission from the author. For information, contact @BrookeandKi

WBM Publishing/Model Shrink, INC.
www.ModelShrink.com

Inspired by true events.

# Brooke & Ki

On a beautiful fall afternoon, Brooke went to visit her aunt. She had a gorgeous Alaskan Husky with icy blue eyes that gazed up at her, as if to say, "Play? Play? Play?" His name was Ki. My aunt confessed with tear-filled eyes that she adored Ki, but she could no longer provide him with the care such an energetic dog needed, and she was looking for someone to care for him. As Brooke watched her aunt's heart break, Brooke just knew that Ki had to be a very special dog.

Brooke & Ki

Brooke & Ki

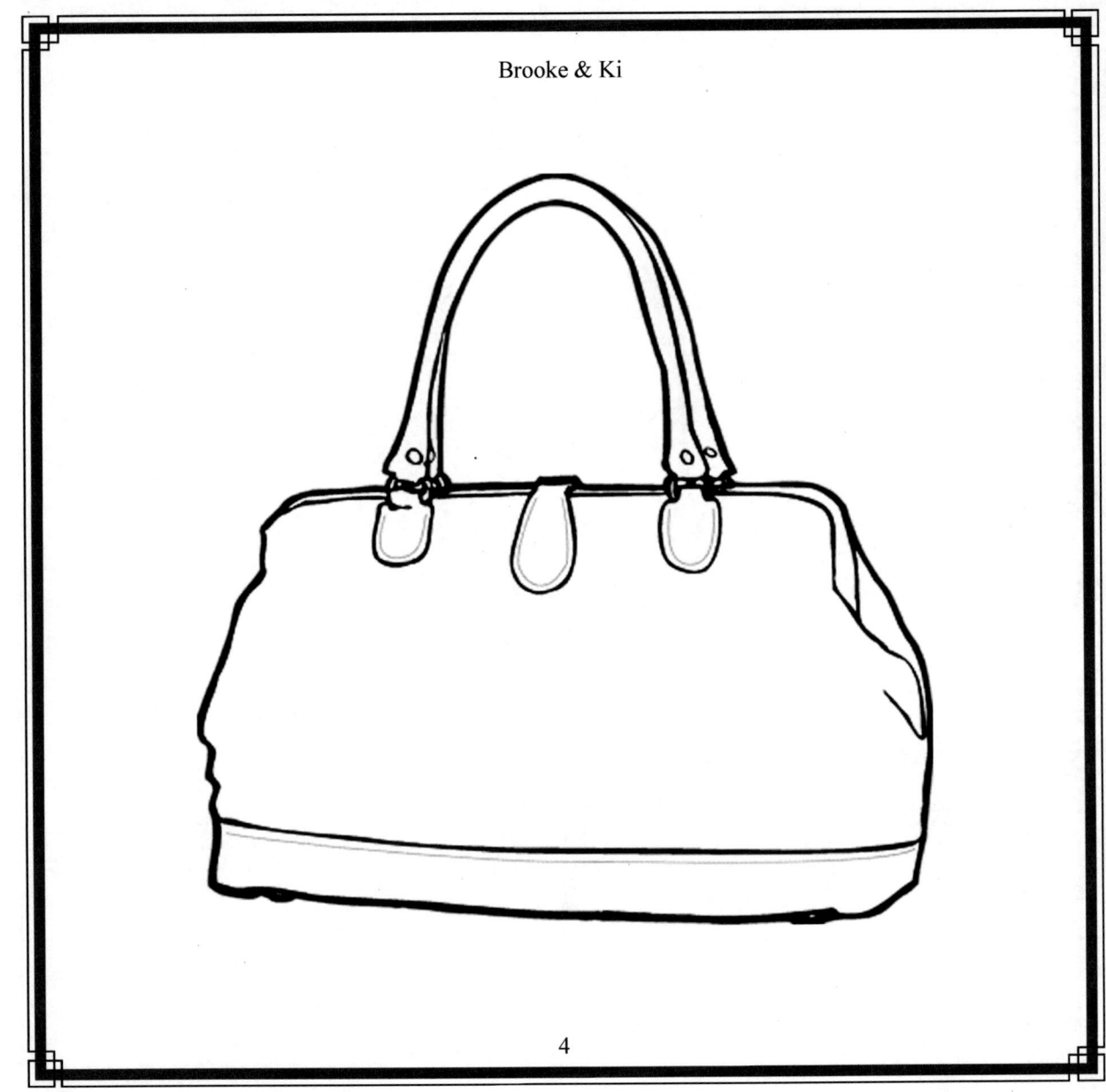

Now Brooke did not exactly have a laid back life. She worked as a **fashion model** in **New York City**. She loved her job and all the pretty clothes she had the chance to wear. And as we all know, most models tote around those cute tiny little dogs in their cute tiny little purses. A husky does not fit in a purse!

Brooke knew her career took up a lot of her time, but sometimes she felt a little lonely. And even though it did not seem like a practical choice, considering that Ki was a puppy and not very well-trained, once he looked up at Brooke with those big blue eyes, she loved Ki. Ki loved her. So, Brooke and her aunt discussed it. Although Brooke was still a little hesitant, she finally agreed.

Brooke & Ki

The next day, Brooke went to pick up Ki. She opened the door and Ki **bounded** right up to her. His tongue was wagging ready to give Brooke sloppy kisses. She laughed and hugged his neck, thinking what a wonderful dog, and how nice it would be to have him greet her this way every time she came home.

She picked up his leash. When Ki saw the leash, he was very excited. He began barking and jumping back and forth on the couches. Brooke tried to catch him, but he jumped out of the way.

"Ki, it is time to go," she said sweetly. He looked up at Brooke with his big blue eyes, thinking once again, "Play? Play? Play?"

She sighed and said firmly, "Time to go!" He jumped over the side of the couch.

"Ki!" Brooke shouted and chased after him. Finally, she snapped the leash on his collar. The moment Ki felt the leash, he tore off in the other direction, yanking the leash out of her hand. Brooke thought, *Okay, he's not used to the leash*. She lunged for him and he jumped back on to the couch. Brooke jumped on to the couch beside him and he jumped off and ran for the stairs.

By this time Brooke was getting really frustrated. "Ki!" Brooke shouted. Brooke chased him up the stairs only to have Ki run right back down the stairs. When Brooke was finally able to grab the leash, she felt like she had run a marathon. Ki, however, looked like he could run a few more marathons, a hike in the mountains, and about 45 minutes on a treadmill before he would even yawn.

As Brooke opened the front door, Ki tugged at the leash and pulled Brooke right out the door. "Now you're ready to go?" Brooke groaned. *Okay, the hard part's done*, she thought.

Brooke led Ki to her car. But when she opened the door, they had another problem. Ki would not get in the back seat. He sat down and stared at Brooke.

Brooke jumped in and out of the car to show Ki how. He blinked. Brooke tried tugging him inside by his collar. He did not budge. Brooke tried giving him a shove on his backside. Ki yawned.

"Get in Ki," Brooke said sweetly. Ki blinked his blue eyes again at Brooke. "Get in Ki," she pleaded and tugged at his leash. He ignored Brooke once again. Finally, Brooke grabbed a burger she had left from lunch and tossed it into the backseat. Ki jumped in happily. Brooke sighed with relief and thought, *Ki really is a lot of work,* as she closed the door.

As Brooke drove back to her apartment in NYC, she wondered how she would sneak Ki inside. *My apartment did not allow pets, but again, I just had to have Ki*, Brooke thought!

When they arrived, Brooke opened the car door, hoping Ki would not give her a hard time about getting out. Instead, he **bolted** right past Brooke. Even though she had the leash in her hand, along with a few bags, she had no control over Ki. He was very strong and **determined** to run. The bags flew up out of Brooke's hands as he dragged her down the **suburban** NYC streets. Leaves were blowing in Brooke's face, her hair was **whipping** all around, while a wild husky was having a grand time! When she finally got control of Ki, Brooke was really worn out.

She managed to get him into the apartment without anyone jumping out and hollering that she had a dog. As soon as the door closed behind her, Brooke **sighed** with relief.

When Ki and Brooke got home that night, Ki was very sweet and things now would be much easier. Brooke was sure. Ki was happy to snuggle with Brooke on the couch. Brooke tried to teach him a few tricks that ended in Brooke sitting instead of Ki, and Brooke rolling around on the floor while Ki stared at her. Brooke gave Ki snacks instead and he licked Brooke's fingers. Brooke giggled and Ki wagged his tail. She forgot all about how hard it had been to get Ki home. Ki was with her, and that was all that mattered. Brooke went to bed that night sure that she would be the best dog owner ever.

The next morning at 7:20 am, Brooke woke up very early in the morning with a smile on her face. Brooke was ready for a special day because she had a big audition. She also was excited to see Ki, who was happy to greet her. It felt nice to have someone so happy to see her and she was ready to take Ki for a walk before her audition. She was determined to be a very responsible dog owner. This time, she grabbed him by the collar before she snapped on Ki's leash.

Feeling good, Brooke **pranced** him up and down the street of her neighborhood for at least 20 minutes. Ki was fairly well behaved; all he did was sniff, no potty! Brooke knew she had to get to her *audition*. She *decided* to take him home. As soon as they stepped inside the apartment, Ki made a puddle right there on Brooke's carpet! She was **horrified**. How gross, how yucky, and she had to clean it up!

When Brooke snapped the leash off him, Ki hung his head as if he knew he had done wrong. Brooke *sighed* and patted Ki's head lightly. She did not want Ki to think that she was mad.

Finally, Brooke had an audition to go to. She was glad to get a break from Ki. She closed the door behind her and skipped down the hallway. By the time she reached the elevator, Ki began barking and howling at the door. Brooke hurried back, as she could not have her neighbors know that she had a dog! Brooke could not find her keys in her model bag, so she ended up dumping everything out on to the floor. Brooke was so frustrated. She was going to be late for her audition and could get kicked out of her apartment, all because she just had to have Ki!

Brooke & Ki

When Brooke finally got the door open, Ki stopped **howling instantly**. He just wanted to be with Brooke. Brooke realized she would have to take Ki with her. Besides, Brooke could not let him leave puddles all over her apartment while she was gone. She might need boots by the time she got back! Plus, Brooke thought, *I wouldn't want to find any \*"mud" either, if you know what I mean. Gross.* Brooke tugged him into the elevator and threw a hamburger into the backseat of her car. Ki jumped in happily.

Ki was on his best behavior as they drove into the city for Brooke's **audition**, but first she had to make a quick stop at her agency.

> \* **What is a metaphor?** A metaphor is a word or phrase that is used to make a comparison between two people, things, animals, or places.
>
> For an example, "mud" is a metaphor for poo.

When Brooke found a parking space, once again she made sure to put Ki's leash on and held him by his collar before she opened the door. He hopped out joyfully, and seemed to be very content. Brooke felt very confident, and as if everything was in control. She felt very special to have such a special dog. *So we had a rough start, how bad could it get?* Brooke thought, as she let go of his collar. Brooke was going to learn that there is one thing that you just don't say, and that is 'how bad could it get?'

Suddenly, Brooke's hair went flying through the air once again as Ki tugged her at full speed down the sidewalk. Her bag was flying in the air and she was rocking back and forth on her fancy heels, trying to keep up. Pictures were fluttering out of her bag as Ki ran faster. Brooke managed to get her balance and wiped her hair out of her face only to discover that Ki was chasing a flock of birds! The crazy dog was trying to eat them!

Brooke & Ki

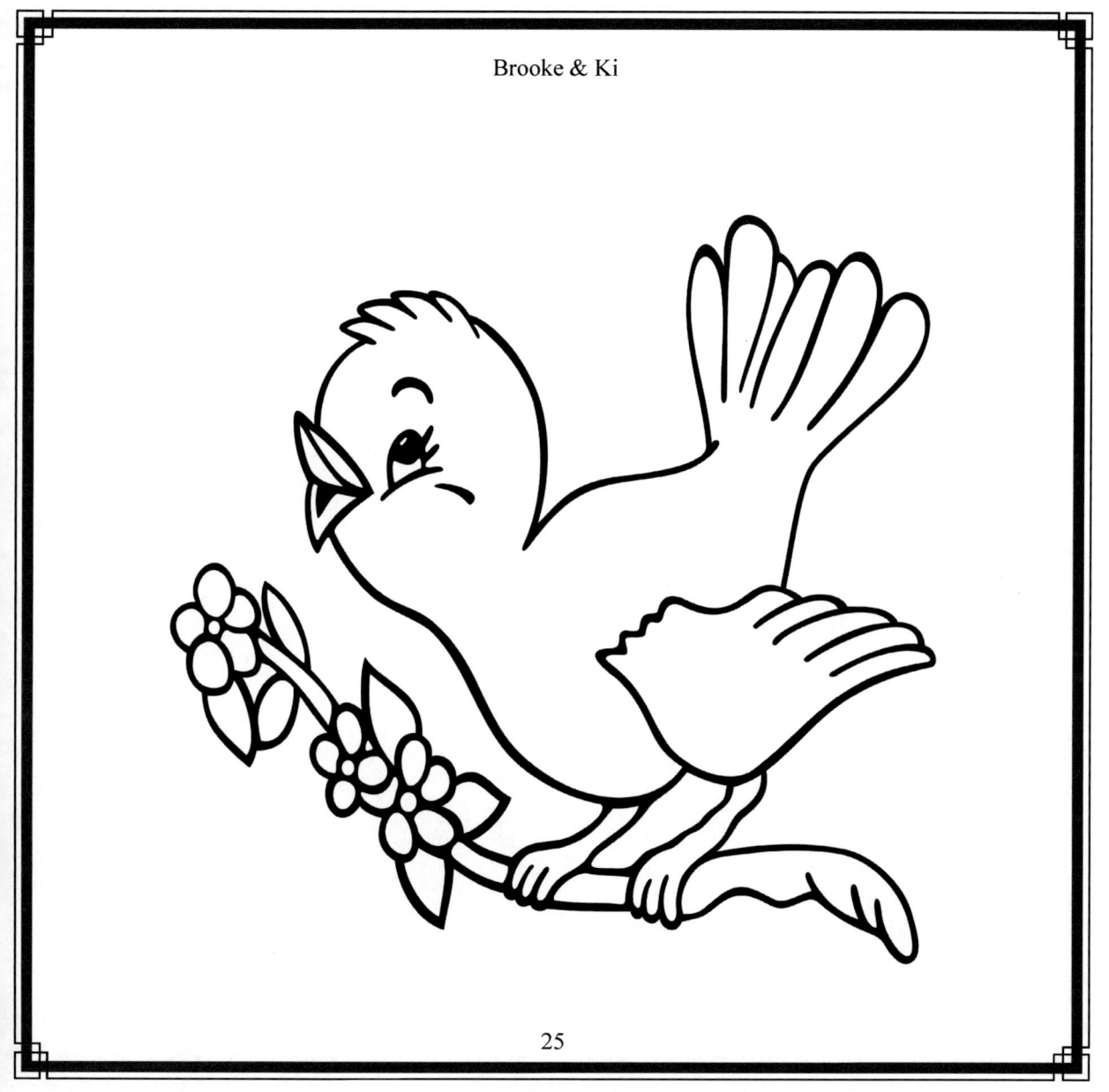

Brooke yanked on his leash hard to try to show him who was in charge. Apparently, he had the same idea because he yanked back just as hard and nearly knocked Brooke off her heels. Every time Brooke pulled hard, he pulled harder, until finally the birds flew away. Ki had ruined her shoes, and scattered the contents of her bag across New York City just to get to some silly birds.

"Ki!" Brooke growled. And after catching her breath, she looked up to find they were in front of her agency.

Everyone that walked by was smiling at Ki. One even made a comment that he was very well-mannered. Brooke rolled her eyes, and thought, *If you only knew*. Brooke was worried about taking Ki into the agency, but she thought, what could he possibly do in an office? Ki was good in the car, and as long as she was with him, he was good in the apartment. And as long as there was not a flock of birds inside, Brooke thought they would be just fine.

Brooke dragged Ki in to the elevator. Ki was great in the elevator up to the agency, but still Brooke had a stern conversation with Ki about behaving. Brooke asked him not to embarrass her in the agency and to try hard to be cute.

When they stepped into the agency, Ki was fine. As soon as Brooke started saying hello to people, Ki started barking very loudly. Agents were on the phone making million dollar deals, and Brooke's dog would not stop barking making it hard to hear! It was like Ki was trying to audition for one of those movies where the dog ruins its owner's life.

Mortified, Brooke hurried Ki back into the elevator. At this point, she was so embarrassed and frustrated that she was at the end of her rope. She turned to Ki and asked, "Why are you doing this to me?" He only continued to bark and howl. She had a very important audition, so she had to leave Ki tied to a post on the sidewalk. Brooke knew he would be safe, but Ki's eyes were very sad when she walked away. Brooke was so angry that she did not care. She spent her entire audition wondering if Ki was the right dog for her.

After a grueling audition, Brooke was exhausted. She returned to find Ki fairly calm, surrounded by people who were petting him. They all said how good of a dog Ki was.

Brooke only shook her head. She was only hoping he would stay calm.

When Brooke got Ki into the car, they drove to a friend's house to drop something off. As Brooke's friend watched her struggle with Ki, she shook her head.

Brooke tried taking him around her other friends, but each one had an excuse not to want to be around Ki. One said Ki was too lively and would break their glass table. Another said Ki was too big and would trample on his fine carpet. Even Brooke's best friend refused to see them, saying that Ki was just too much to handle, as she said on the phone one day, "That dog is dumb." Brooke was mad and came to Ki's defense. Brooke said, "Ki is not dumb. He sure is a pain, but he is not dumb!" It was the first time Brooke realized how **protective** she was of Ki. He had become like a best friend no matter how **annoying** his habits were….well, until he sneaked a quick bite.

Brooke & Ki

They were riding in the elevator up to her apartment, and it felt like he bit Brooke's leg!

"Oh no! You did not just bite me!" Brooke hollered as the elevator doors opened, her landlord waiting outside her door. Brooke was worried, but he did not seem to care that she had Ki with her. Ki was bouncing around wanting attention, while Brooke's landlord explained that he needed to fix a wire inside the apartment. As soon as she opened the door, Ki urinated on the landlord's shoe.

"Oh, I am so sorry. He is just a puppy," Brooke said as she struggled to hold on to Ki. "No matter how long I walk him, he always waits to **urinate** in the apartment. Unfortunately, you are stepping in that spot."

Brooke tried to settle Ki down by asking him to sit. Ki of course refused. "I just can't control him." Brooke's landlord said, "Sit!" and that dog sat right down. Brooke was shocked and impressed. She asked the landlord how he did that. The landlord explained he had cared for several dogs at home and was used to training them. The landlord could see that Ki needs some training. "With the right amount of time and a good schedule he will be just fine," her landlord said.

Brooke's tears were falling swiftly. "I just don't have enough time," she admitted. "My life is very busy."

That moment, Brooke realized maybe Ki was too much dog for her to handle. Maybe she was not able to care or train him the way he needed to be trained. On top of that, Brooke was very sad, and missed her friends. She had thought having a dog would be fun, but it had turned out to be a much bigger responsibility than she had ever expected.

It was a hard decision, but Brooke knew Ki and her were just not a good fit.

"I have no choice but to give Ki back to my aunt," she said to the landlord.

The landlord nodded and smiled, "It's okay. I can help you. We will work together, and Ki will be trained in no time."

Brooke was so happy to have run into her landlord. She did not know if the training would be enough, but she was glad that Ki had someone he would listen to. She knew now that getting a dog was more than just having a new friend; it was a responsibility that she had to make room for in her life.

Brooke & Ki

Made in the USA
Columbia, SC
27 May 2017